BY KATHRYN WALTON

VISIT AMERICA'S NATIONAL PARKS!

VISIT GREAT SMOKY MOUNTAINS NATIONAL PARK!

Enslow PUBLISHING

Please visit our website, www.enslow.com. For a free color catalog of all our high-quality books, call toll free 1-800-398-2504 or fax 1-877-980-4454.

Library of Congress Cataloging-in-Publication Data

Names: Walton, Kathryn, 1993- author.
Title: Visit Great Smoky Mountains National Park! / Kathryn Walton.
Description: Buffalo, NY : Enslow Publishing, 2025. | Series: Visit America's national parks! | Includes index.
Identifiers: LCCN 2024004357 (print) | LCCN 2024004358 (ebook) | ISBN 9781978540637 (library binding) | ISBN 9781978540620 (paperback) | ISBN 9781978540644 (ebook)
Subjects: LCSH: Great Smoky Mountains (N.C. and Tenn.)–Juvenile literature.
Classification: LCC F443.G7 W358 2025 (print) | LCC F443.G7 (ebook) | DDC 976.8/89–dc23/eng/20240213
LC record available at https://lccn.loc.gov/2024004357
LC ebook record available at https://lccn.loc.gov/2024004358

Published in 2025 by
Enslow Publishing
2544 Clinton Street
Buffalo, NY 14224

Portions of this work were originally authored by Santana Hunt and published as *Great Smoky Mountains National Park*. All new material in this edition is authored by Kathryn Walton.

Designer: Tanya Dellaccio Keeney
Editor: Natalie Humphrey

Photo credits: Series Art (illustration) khezy licious/Shutterstock.com; cover (photo). p. 11 (bottom) Sean Pavone/Shutterstock.com; p. 5 Emaps/Shutterstock.com; p. 7 (top) Mihai_Andritoiu/Shutterstock/com; p. 7 (bottom) Kyle S Lo/Shutterstock.com; p. 9 (top) Ben McMurtray/Shutterstock.com; p. 9 (bottom) ewjohnson00/Shutterstock.com; p. 11 (top) Peter Turner Photography/Shutterstock.com; p. 13 (top) BlueBarronPhoto/Shutterstock.com; p. 13 (bottom) Steve Byland/Shutterstock.com; p. 15 Kelly vanDellen/Shutterstock.com; p. 17 Jeff McCord/Shutterstoc.com; p. 19 Chansak Joe/Shutterstock.com.

Printed in the United States of America

CPSIA compliance information: Batch #CSENS25: For further information contact Enslow Publishing at 1-800-398-2504.

CONTENTS

WELCOME TO GREAT SMOKY MOUNTAINS NATIONAL PARK 4
THE CHEROKEE 6
MANY SPECIES 8
TREES, TREES, AND MORE TREES 10
WATCH FOR ANIMALS! 12
BLACK BEARS AND SALAMANDERS 14
MANY WATERFALLS 16
THE HIGHEST TOWER 18
TIMING YOUR VISIT 20
GLOSSARY 22
FOR MORE INFORMATION 23
INDEX 24

Words in the glossary appear in **bold** type the first time they are used in the text.

WELCOME TO GREAT SMOKY MOUNTAINS NATIONAL PARK

There's a lot to do and see in Great Smoky Mountains National Park. The Great Smoky Mountains are part of the western Appalachian Mountains. Many people enjoy hiking, fishing, horseback riding, or camping in these mountains. In fact, Great Smoky Mountains National Park is the most visited national park in the United States!

Join the more than 10 million people who travel to this beautiful national park each year and find out what makes it a perfect stop on any trip.

MORE TO KNOW

Great Smoky Mountains National Park was established in 1934. The park **protects** the plants and animals living there.

Great Smoky Mountains National Park is in eastern Tennessee and western North Carolina.

THE CHEROKEE

The Cherokee people have been living in the Great Smokies for more than 1,000 years. They named the Great Smoky Mountains the "place of blue smoke" because of the blue haze, or fog, that surrounds the area.

In the 1700s, white settlers arrived in the area. During the 1830s, the United States increasingly wanted to take over land the Cherokee lived on. The Cherokee people fought back, but most were forced out of their homes by the U.S. military.

CHEROKEE, NORTH CAROLINA, HOME OF THE EASTERN BAND OF THE CHEROKEE NATION

The Eastern Band of the Cherokee Nation still lives near the border of Great Smoky Mountains National Park.

MORE TO KNOW

The Cherokee people were forced to move west by the U.S. government. So many people died during this journey that it was called the Trail of Tears.

MANY SPECIES

Many different plant and animal **species** live in Great Smoky Mountains National Park. Scientists know of more than 19,000 species of plants and animals living in the park.

The park's special **ecosystem** helps it support so many different plants and animals. Weather at the higher elevations in the park is cooler and wetter than in the land around it. Animals and plants that like the cooler weather live higher in the Smokies. Those that like the warm weather can be found below.

Scientists believe there may be more than 80,000 species living in the park that haven't been discovered yet!

BLACK BEARS

MORE TO KNOW

The Great Smoky Mountains are one of the oldest mountain ranges in the United States.

BLUEBIRD

TREES, TREES, AND MORE TREES

Most of Great Smoky Mountains National Park is covered in trees. Some of these trees have been around for thousands of years! The park is home to more than 130 tree species, more than any other U.S. park. That's almost as many tree species as in all of Europe!

Hemlocks, spruces, and other trees grow tall in the park. The forest is so **dense** in some spots that it may be hard to spot wildlife!

MORE TO KNOW

If you take a trip to the park, make sure to bring an umbrella. At the highest point in the park, it rains around 85 inches (216 cm) each year!

BLACK GUM TREE LEAVES

The oldest tree in the Great Smoky Mountains is a black gum tree that's more than 560 years old.

WATCH FOR ANIMALS!

Many species of birds make their nests in Great Smoky Mountains National Park. Black-capped chickadees, Canada warblers, and winter wrens can be found there. The cerulean warbler, and some other birds in the park, have become uncommon as their numbers decrease.

About 65 species of **mammals** live in the park. You can try to spot white-tailed deer, raccoons, and woodchucks. The Carolina northern flying squirrel and the Indiana bat are two **endangered** mammals that can be found in the park.

Many animals in Great Smoky Mountains National Park are most active at night, such as these white-tailed deer.

BLACK-CAPPED CHICKADEE

MORE TO KNOW

There have been about 240 species of birds seen in the park. Only around 60 of them live in the park year-round.

BLACK BEARS AND SALAMANDERS

Have you ever seen a black bear? You might be able to spot one in Great Smoky Mountains National Park! About 1,500 American black bears live there. The park is the largest natural protected area for these bears.

The park also has many salamanders living in it. Great Smoky Mountains National Park has at least 30 species of salamanders living in it!

Great Smoky Mountains National Park has so many salamanders, it is sometimes called the salamander capital of the world!

MORE TO KNOW

Of the many salamanders that live in the park, 24 species don't have lungs! They mostly breathe through their skin.

MANY WATERFALLS

If you take a trip to Great Smoky Mountains National Park, make sure you see the many waterfalls in the park! There are several trails around the park that lead to these amazing sites.

The 80-foot (24.4-m) tall Laurel Falls gets its name from the mountain laurel, a plant that blooms near the falls in the spring. Hen Wallow Falls is 90 feet (27.4 m) high and may freeze during the winter. You can also stop by Abrams Falls and Grotto Falls during your trip.

MORE TO KNOW

The tallest waterfall in Great Smoky Mountains National Park is Ramsey Cascades. This waterfall is 100 feet (30.5 m) tall!

Visitors who want to see the Ramsey Cascades will have to hike at least 4 miles (6.4 km) to get to the falls.

RAMSEY CASCADES

THE HIGHEST TOWER

The highest point in the park is Clingmans **Dome** in Tennessee. This peak is 6,643 feet (2,024.5 m) high. The top of it can be hard for some to reach. You can drive most of the way, but the road ends in a very steep walk to a tower at the top.

Another steep hike is the Chimney Tops Trail. The trail is shorter, but the end is so steep that many people don't make it to the top!

The tower at Clingmans Dome is usually closed from December to late March.

MORE TO KNOW

In 2022, The Eastern Band of Cherokee began working to change the name of Clingmans Dome back to its original Cherokee name: Kuwohi.

TIMING YOUR VISIT

Great Smoky Mountains National Park is open year-round, but some seasons may be better to visit in than others. June through August is the best time to see wildlife in the park. During the fall, you can see the leaves change color!

November through March is the time to go if you want to see the mountains covered in snow. No matter what season, this national park is a great place to visit!

MORE TO KNOW

If you want to avoid crowds, the best months to see the park are March through May.

GREAT SMOKY MOUNTAINS NATIONAL PARK

THE FACTS

ESTABLISHED
1934

SIZE
816 square miles (2,113 sq km)

NUMBER OF VISITORS EACH YEAR
over 10 million

NATIVE WILDLIFE
foxes, wild turkeys, black bears, white-tailed deer, and more

NATIVE PLANTS
hemlocks, azaleas, black walnuts, white-blossomed rhododendrons, and more

MUST-SEE STOPS
Appalachian National Scenic Trail, Clingmans Dome, Blue Ridge Parkway

GLOSSARY

dense: Packed very closely together.

dome: A mountain with a rounded top.

ecosystem: A natural community of life that includes living and nonliving features.

endangered: In danger of dying out.

mammal: A warm-blooded animal that has a backbone and hair, breathes air, and feeds milk to its young.

protect: To keep safe.

species: A group of plants or animals that are all the same kind.

FOR YOUR INFORMATION

Books

Bowman, Chris. *Great Smoky Mountains National Park.* Minneapolis, MN: 2023.

Perritano, John. *Great Smoky Mountains.* New York, NY: AV2, 2021.

Websites

National Geographic Kids: Great Smoky Mountains National Park
kids.nationalgeographic.com/nature/article/greatsmokymountains
Learn more about the history of Great Smoky Mountains National Park.

National Park Service: Great Smoky Mountains
www.nps.gov/grsm/learn/kidsyouth/index.htm
Find out more things you can do during your trip to the park.

INDEX

Abrams Falls, 16
Appalachian Mountains, 4
black bears, 14, 21
Cherokee, 6, 7, 19
Chimney Tops Trail, 18
Clingmans Dome, 18, 19, 21
endangered species, 12
Grotto Falls, 16
hike, 4, 16, 18
Hen Wallow Falls, 16
Laurel Falls, 16
North Carolina, 5
Ramsey Cascades, 17
salamanders, 14, 15
Tennessee, 5, 18
Trail of Tears, 7
trees, 10, 11
weather, 8, 11, 20
wildlife, 8, 9, 10, 12, 20, 21